Crisis Management Handbook

A Quick Reference Guide for Meeting Planners

Debi Scholar and **Susan Losurdo**

Scholar
Consulting
Group, LLC

Trusted Advisors and Superior Solutions
for the Travel and Meetings Market

Barrel Maker Publishing
2013

Table of Contents

Endorsements

If you've been putting off preparing your own Crisis Management Plan, Scholar Consulting Group has given you a head start! Complete the Appendix pages to make them your own, and take the time to put your full plan together...*before* you need it!

Carolyn Pund, CMP, CMM
Senior Manager, Global Strategic Meetings Management

Debi Scholar is a true master when it comes to all things SMMP. She was one of the original thought leaders that helped to develop the now industry accepted standard SMMP roadmap for corporations and procurement groups. Her attention to details and total understanding of the important mechanics for meetings and events is impressively on display in this Crisis Management Guide. I predict it will become the go-to publication and guide for all meeting and event planners who want to be 100% knowledgeable and covered when planning corporate meetings and events. I highly recommend Debi's Crisis Management Guide as a critical investment for all professionals in our industry and marketplace.

Kevin Iwamoto, GLP & GTP
Vice President, Industry Strategy
ACTIVE Network

Debi Scholar and Susan Losurdo's handbook is well organized, carefully prepared and covers all conceivable aspects of crisis management. This book is an excellent resource to meeting planners. It is thorough!

Adele Gianino, CMP
Director, Meetings & Travel
The Catholic Health Association of the United States

Such an important tool that should be in every meeting planner's office when planning and executing a meeting! Whether it is a Board meeting or a citywide convention, this information is invaluable, yet few planners have anything this detailed. Thank you Debi and Susan for your expertise in compiling this fabulous book.

Deborah Borak, CDS, SMMC
Director of Global Accounts
ConferenceDirect

Great topic and as usual you have clearly defined the importance of identifying, preparing and executing to plan. Useful ideas and updated processes that are easy to implement into existing plans. Many planners that I speak to do not give enough attention to this critical area. Your handbook will be a great add to their tool kit and one that I will be adding into our ongoing training schedule! Fantastic work Debi and Susan!

Jana Atlas, CMP
Vice President, Global Conferences & Events
FROSCH

Finally! A handbook that breaks this down into categories and checklists, complete with useable templates. This is how planners think. I've taken many classes on this subject but the information was always vague because it was more about the <u>concept</u> of preparedness vs. <u>implementation</u>. This is tactical and will be a part of our SMMP training to our planners

Victoria Johnson, CMP, CMM
Global Manager, Meeting Services & Sourcing
Underwriters Laboratories Inc.

Acknowledgements

In my first book, the acknowledgements section was a book in itself. Since then, my wonderful cheerleader, anchor, rock, and best friend has left me—mom. Mom planned many events as the Unit Chairperson of UAW Local 19 in Grand Rapids, Michigan and her attention to detail was passed on to me. Mom always told me to "stand up for what you believe in" and to this day, I follow her orders. Since she left me on April 3, 2012 writing and working has helped fill the void of not being with her every day. Miss and love you, Mom.

Laurynn and Justin, my wonderful children, continue reaching for the stars. I'm so proud of all of your accomplishments. Berklee College of Music produced the best music therapist on this planet and New York University will be producing one of the best film professionals. Thanks to my husband, David, for supporting all of my efforts over the years.

Susan, you are a best friend, hard-worker, and a superstar. I love watching you put your heart and soul into a project, and you are always a huge success; I am so grateful that you are part of my life and business. Thank you for helping me with this book.

I don't think I could have made it through this past year without my best girlfriends. These women helped me make it through the toughest year of my life: Deb Einig Lamb, Corinne Snow, Krista Stressman, Deborah Borak, Kim McGlinn, and Susan Losurdo ….thank you, thank you, thank you for being there for me and listening to all of my craziness. Marie Maldonado – my new sister and best friend, we formed a new bond through mom and I am so happy we have each other. Last, but not least, thanks to Kevin Iwamoto who has been a best friend and mentor. You have been my compass for many years. Thank you.

I wrote my first rhyme when I was 6 or 7 years old. Since then, I have written hundreds of short rhymes; enjoy this one as it relates to Crisis Management.

Crisis Management In Action

Deep into drills, we pushed our way through.

Orders and briefings, we learned what to do.

News of the crisis shocked our day.

Mayhem among us, we started to pray.

Action in Command Center, we took control,

The planners in charge, we knew our goal.

Hotel staff and FEMA support began,

Embracing the start of our Crisis Management Plan.

What do we do, where do we go?

Successful risk training, we're in the know.

By Debi Scholar

Debi Scholar and Susan Losurdo

Through every one of life's crisis' - we have held each other's hand and carried each other through. Together, anything is possible.

You are my love, my best friend, my heart, my soul.

"I'll meet you any time you want, in our Italian Restaurant" (lyrics by Billy Joel)

By Susan Losurdo

About the Authors

Debi Scholar, President of Scholar Consulting Group (SCG), is a consultant, strategist, speaker, educator, and author. Her "10,000 foot level" vision and her operational "roll up your sleeves approach" steers her passion for delivering exceptional quality service to her Clients who experience up to 25% savings, up to 75% risk reduction, and for those Clients that are suppliers, up to 300% increase in sales. Debi supports hundreds of corporate and association clients with their meetings and events, travel, card, expense, and training programs.

She authored Strategic Meetings Management (SMM): The Quick Reference Guide and co-authored The SMM Handbook. With eight designations, she is driven to constantly improve her expertise so that she can implement best practices with her clients. Debi created the industry's first SMM Maturity Model©, her must-read blog, T&E Plus, has been viewed over 40,000 times, and her T&E Plus LinkedIn Group has over 2,000 members. She also created the GBTA SMM LinkedIn Group that has over 1,000 members.

Before starting her own consultancy, Debi managed the PricewaterhouseCooper's (PwC) SMM Program and she was the first Meeting Director to have included Virtual Meetings under her direction back in 2002. She is a meeting strategist bridging the meeting content, architecture, and theming into successful, measurable meetings and events. Because she owned her own training company, was a Training Director at PwC, and a Training Manager at Dean Witter, Debi integrates all of her content development training skills along with logistics planning skills which brings multiple benefits to her Clients.

Debi was co-chair of the GBTA Groups & Meetings Committee, a GBTA Foundation Board member, an MCAF member, one of the top 20 Changemakers in the Industry, and one of the VIPs in the Strategic Meetings Management Industry.

Debi has the following designations Global Business Travel Association (GBTA) Global Leadership Professional (GLP), Global Travel Professional (GTP), Corporate Travel Expert (CTE), Certificate in Meetings Management (CMM), Certified Meeting Professional (CMP), Six Sigma Green Belt (SSGB), Certified Technical Trainer (CTT), and Certified BANK™ Sales Trainer (CBST).

Debi can be reached at 1-908-304-4954 or at Debi@DebiScholar.com.

Susan N Losurdo, CMP, LES is a Global Meeting & Event Management Professional with over 15 years of extensive experience as both a Corporate Meeting Manager, Planner and a Hotel Supplier.

Currently, Susan has taken on the role of Vice President at The Scholar Consulting Group (SCG). Her main function is to oversee the Meeting & Event Operations arm of the Group by managing seamless events for SCG clients. At a higher level - Susan understands and promotes the Strategic Meetings Management Program (SMMP) philosophy. She uses this knowledge to analyze and compile client meeting data in order to provide organizations a better understanding of how SMMP can benefit them. Susan has co-authored the "Meeting & Event Planning Playbook" as well as a "Crisis Management Guide". She speaks and instructs at the university level on topics related to hospitality and event management.

Prior to her work at The Scholar Consulting Group, Susan had the opportunity to learn and excel in various other meeting management roles. She has worked as a corporate meeting planner (Global Meeting & Event Manager - PricewaterhouseCoopers, LLP) and as a third party meeting planner (Experient - Onsite at Cisco

Technologies - Manager, Meeting & Event Operations - Team Lead North America). Susan even worked as a meeting supplier (Hyatt Hotels - Sales, Catering, and Convention Services). This breadth of experience positions her well to understand various perspectives and partner well with her clients.

Planning meetings and events from end-to-end, managing teams, mentoring and training staff, reporting, consulting, teaching, writing ... all are things Susan is passionate about.

Susan is a member of Meeting Professionals International (MPI) as well as International Association of Protocol Consultants (IAPC). She holds a Bachelor of Business Administration degree in Marketing from the University of Wisconsin - Madison.

Susan holds the following professional designations: Certified Meeting Professional (CMP) and Learning Environmental Specialist (LES)

Susan can be reached at salosurdo@gmail.com.

How to Use this Handbook

1. As a Quick Reference Guide in your briefcase, Smartphone, and Tablet

2. As a method to begin conversations among your team members about your Crisis Management Plans

3. As a supplement to your Crisis Management Plan training / education

Introduction

Disasters, whether they be natural or human-caused, can be a traumatic for all of us, and especially for Meeting Planners who often have a Plan A, Plan B, and Plan C. Yet, nothing quite prepares us for everything that may go wrong onsite.

A recent survey found that 36% of Meeting Planners do not have Crisis Management Standard Operating Procedures (SOPs) in place. A crisis can be crippling, yet the best Meeting Planners will prepare for crises and ensure that processes, resources, and technology are all in place to support their meetings and events.

The purpose of this **Crisis Management Handbook** is to provide you with guidelines that may be followed in an emergency. At **all** times, the official emergency personnel and organization's Security Team instructions will supersede these guidelines.

YOUR processes may be very different than the procedures offered in this Handbook. Make notes on the blank pages as to the procedures of your organization. Our hope is that this Handbook will start the crisis management discussion in your organization if it has not been held in the past.

1. Carry this handbook with you in a hard copy format and electronic format on your smartphone, iPad, computer, and other devices.

2. Keep contact information, phone numbers, and other important information in multiple places, including both hard copy and electronic versions.

3. Meeting Planners who are onsite at meetings are usually expected to have their computers / iPads with them at all times, their phone turned on at all times, and be prepared to take control during times of crises. If a crisis occurs in

the middle of the night, and a computer is locked in a meeting room that may not be accessible, then important data may not be available. When possible, data should be replicated locally to the hard drive so that if the Internet is not available, the Meeting Planners will still have access to important data. Moreover, important reports should be printed before going onsite because technology may not last long without power. And, printers may not be available.

4. Be flexible and try to remain calm.

This Handbook is, however, too brief to cover every situation that you may face as a Meeting Planner. To help you prepare for all types of incidents, additional sources of information have been included. One of the best guides is the Federal Emergency Management Agency's 204-page "**Are You Ready: An In-Depth Guide to Citizen Preparedness**."

Throughout this Handbook, the term "Meeting Planner" refers to the professional or ad-hoc person(s) who is onsite and in charge of the meeting logistics.

Four-Step Risk Mitigation Model

There is a four-step process that every Meeting Planner should go through when preparing for a meeting or event. It includes mitigation, preparedness, response, and recovery.

Mitigation means that the Meeting Planner should try to avoid the potential risk exposure altogether, although this is not always possible.

Preparedness means that the Meeting Planner should always plan for crises, and there are numerous sorts of crises that may occur. Role playing is an excellent method to learn how to prepare for crises.

Response means that the Meeting Planner will have to use his or her Crisis Management Plan and Emergency Toolkits to address the crisis head-on.

Recovery means that the Meeting Planner should debrief and determine what processes, technology, or resources must be improved to be better equipped for the next crisis.

Four Step Model to Crisis Management

	Mitigate	Prepare	
Types of Crisis 1. Geological (earthquakes, volcanos, etc.) 2. Meteorological (floods, snow, tornados, hurricanes, etc.) 3. Biological (foodborne illnesses, allergies, heart attacks, etc.) 4. Human-caused accidental or intentional (e.g. nuclear power, fires, explosions, robbery, lost person, bomb, suicide, terrorism, etc.) 5. Technological (e.g. utility / tele-communications interruption or failure)	• Eliminate or decrease risk exposure • Consider putting policies or controls in place to decrease risk • Communicate with leaders and attendees; share best practices in risk mitigation in terms of crisis management • Ensure that the meeting resources are properly skilled • Ensure that the right locations, suppliers, and contracts are in place	• Prepare for multiple scenarios including the worst case scenario in all areas of focus • Identify the threats: know the strengths • Team with key stakeholders to gain perspective on risk and take proactive measures (plans, toolkits, emergency packages, etc.) • Put controls in place to reduce risk exposure proactively	} Proactive

	Respond	Recover	
Types of Crisis 1. Geological (earthquakes, volcanos, etc.) 2. Meteorological (floods, snow, tornados, hurricanes, etc.) 3. Biological (foodborne illnesses, allergies, heart attacks, etc.) 4. Human-caused accidental or intentional (e.g. nuclear power, fires, explosions, robbery, lost person, bomb, suicide, terrorism, etc.) 5. Technological (e.g. utility / tele-communications interruption or failure)	• Take immediate action in all affected focus areas • Evaluate non-affected areas to determine if actions must be taken • Take immediate action by redeploying resources as necessary to assist • Use the Crisis Management Plan and Toolkit • Check controls to determine if they worked	• Determine how to move forward • Debrief; identify lessons learned and transfer the knowledge to all • Review frequently and practice through role plays for each risk exposure scenario as necessary	} Reactive

© Debi Scholar 2010

Risk Impact Analysis

For important meetings, it is recommended that the Meeting Planner and meeting requester use a Risk Impact Analysis, which is a method to score your meeting / event based on several factors such as location, roles and levels of attendees, content sensitivity, off-site activities, duration of meeting, and many other components.

A Risk Impact Analysis measures the impact and the probability of occurrence using a rating scale. If the total score is less than 300, then there is a low risk. If the score is between 301 and 600, then there is a medium risk exposure, and over 601, the meeting is deemed a high risk exposure.

If a meeting is scored at a medium or high rating, then additional services may be implemented such as hired security, more staff, etc.

If you would like more information on how to conduct a Risk Impact Analysis score for your meetings or events, please contact Debi Scholar.

Debi's Risk Analysis Factors for Meetings

Debi uses a method that a) lists all of the key risk exposure factors for each meeting, b) identifies the impact that each risk has on the meeting, and c) estimates the probability that the risk will occur. The result is a *Meeting Risk Analysis Score*. Below are only two examples of the numerous risk exposure factors on the Risk Analysis Scorecard.

Calculate Impact **and** Probability

- People (level, quantity, role)
- Crisis Exposure based on FEMA outline
- Meeting / Event activities
- Process / Technology

Map Score Results

- Low Risk Score <300
- Medium Risk Score 301 - 600
- High Risk Score >600

People Risk Exposure (example)	
Who will be attending?	
Board, CEO, Vice Chairs	9 (high risk)
VPs, Leadership Committee	5
Directors	3
None of the above	1 (low risk)

Location Risk Exposure (example)	
What is the Location Risk Rating?	
Severe (e.g. travel to location not recommended)	9
High	5
Medium	3
Low	1

Figure 1 - Example of Risk Impact Analysis Scorecard

Types of Crises That May Occur

Meeting Planners cannot possibly plan for every type of crisis, as the government highlights[1], but there are some standard preparations that a planner can make. The hazards are divided into two major categories: natural and human-caused events. In each of those categories, there are subcategories.

Natural Hazards

Geological hazards

- Earthquake
- Tsunami
- Volcano
- Landslide, mudslide, subsidence

Meteorological hazards

- Flood, flash flood, tidal surge
- Water control structure / dam levee failure
- Drought
- Snow, ice, hail, sleet, arctic freeze
- Windstorm, tropical cyclone, hurricane, tornado, dust storm
- Extreme temperatures (heat, cold)
- Lightning strikes (fires following, power outages, etc.)

Biological hazards

- Foodborne illnesses
- Individual hazards (allergic reactions, heart attacks, etc.)

---

1   U.S. Government "Emergency Response Plan" www.ready.gov/business

- Pandemic / infectious / communicable disease (Avian flu, H1N1, etc.)

Technology-caused event

- Utility interruption or failure (telecommunications, electrical power, water, gas, HVAC, pollution control system, sewerage system, other critical infrastructure)

Human-caused events (accidental and intentional)

Accidental

- Hazardous material spill or release
- Nuclear power plant incident
- Explosion / fire
- Transportation accident
- Building / structure collapse
- Entrapment and / or rescue (machinery, confined space, high angle, water)
- Transportation Incidents (motor vehicle, railroad, watercraft, aircraft, pipeline)

Intentional

- Robbery
- Lost person, child abduction, kidnap, extortion, hostage incident, workplace violence, suicide attempts, incarcerations
- Demonstration, civil disturbance
- Bomb threat, suspicious package
- Terrorism

Preplanning - Before the Meeting / Event

Policy vs. Guidelines

As a Meeting Planner, it is important to understand the difference between the organization's meeting, travel, or T&E policy(s) vs. guidelines. Policies are meant to be followed whereas guidelines are recommendations.

Whether the organization uses policies or guidelines, we will use the term "policy" throughout this Handbook. In a time of crisis, the safety and security of people are the primary concerns. Still, a Meeting Planner should be aware of and understand policies that are in place that may affect meetings. These policies may be:

- Travel and Entertainment (T&E) Expense Policy
- Meeting and Events Policy
- Code of Conduct Policy
- Procurement Policy
- And many others

For example, a policy may offer the procedures to follow if there is an automobile accident with a rental car, or the process to follow for stolen or lost computers.

Contracts

Not all hotel properties or other venues will provide you with their crisis management plans; however, you may add the following two paragraphs to your contract to encourage them to share as much as possible with you:

- Hotel or venue shall provide a detailed copy of its crisis management plan, safety and security measures, and / or equipment including but not limited to: the opportunity to review a Hotel's fire safety and evacuation plans; the availability of backup generators in the event of power failure; ambulance and paramedic availability either on site or having a contract relationship with the Hotel or venue; contract security guard presence in the Hotel or venue by number and hours covered; name and contact numbers for the Hotel Security / Fire Safety Director; location and numbers of closed caption television ("CCTV") cameras in Hotel or venue and parking areas; confirmation that the CCTV cameras are monitored in real time or that video is stored for possible follow-up after an incident; and the history of theft and other criminal activity on Hotel or venue property.

- Hotel or venue will agree to have hard-wired smoke detectors, carbon monoxide detectors, and sprinklers in each guest room and room(s) where the meeting will be taking place, an automated external defibrillator (AED), and an epi-pen onsite and available for use for attendee well-being. The number of AEDs, and their locations, should align with the size of the entire Hotel or venue according to the guidelines set forth by the U.S. Department of Health and Human Services.

Ask your Hotel or venue if they have tested their emergency management plans by using the basic government standards at http://www.ready.gov/business.

Working with the Hotel or Venue before going onsite to your meeting / event:

1. Send the form that is in Attachment A to the Hotel or venue so that they may complete the information and you can add it to your Crisis Management Plan.

2. Decide if you will have a staff office at the Hotel or venue, which may end up being a room that is the center of activity during a time of crisis. Some companies title this room as the "War Room," "Mission Control Room," or "Control Room" during times of crisis. For simplicity, we will call it the *Control Room* throughout this Handbook. A Control Room is used in times of emergency except in the case of evacuation. If there is an evacuation, then the meeting planner may need to create a new Control Room that acts as a central location for operations during the crisis. A staff office / Control Room should have working land lines, Internet connectivity, power and power strips, a printer / copier, desks and chairs, lights, water, food, and emergency kits (described below). In addition, the staff office / Control Room should include all of the reports that a meeting planner may need such as contracts, air arrival and departure manifests, rooming lists, and contact phone numbers. If power is out, it is critical that all of these documents be hard copy in addition to being on a computer.

Working with the Travel Management Company before going onsite to your meeting / event:

1. Know who to reach out to at the Travel Management Company to obtain a manifest of travelers. Ensure that you know who will be available 24 / 7, the telephone number, and how quickly they will be able to run reports for you.

Your Role as a Meeting Planner

1. The plans that you may need to prepare for include:

   a. Evacuation Plan

   b. Sheltering Plan (e.g. weather, tornado, etc.)

   c. Shelter-in-Place Plan (e.g. outside airborne hazard)

    d. Lockdown Plan

    e. Medical Emergency Plan

    f. Fire Emergency Plan

The following information will help you put together the right plan based on the type of crisis you may encounter.

2. Create your Crisis Management Plan and Emergency Toolkit

Crisis Management Plan Binder

a. Add the Crisis Management Team Process to your binder. If a process is not in place, use the guidelines in this Handbook to create a process.

b. List the organization's Crisis Management conference call number and ensure that it is available in hard copy and electronic format. Many organizations use a reoccurring teleconference number during times of crisis.

c. Include the completed Onsite Crisis Management Contact sheet as shown in Attachment A.

d. Print the crisis management plans received from Hotel or venue.

e. Include the Important Numbers as identified in Attachment B.

f. Include blank copies of the Incident Report form as shown in Attachment C.

g. Include the sample scripts that can be tailored based on the crisis as shown in Attachment D. Note that your Communications Leader may write and distribute all communications; these are provided as samples only. The Meeting Planner may or may not be in a position to write formal crisis awareness communications to attendees and is usually not in the position to write formal crisis awareness communications to the public.

h. Reports that may be needed include:

    i. Group rooming list

    ii. Air manifests / attendee drive reports

    iii. List of attendees with special needs / disabilities

i. Map of the vicinity

j. Emergency contact information and special needs / disabilities of your attendees, guests, and staff

k. Determine if onsite medical staff will be needed; many meetings include these important resources that become a key resource who will work directly with you and your team.

l. Share the Crisis Management Plan information with Hotel or venue security and other key staff as necessary for their review to identify other items that may need to be included.

Emergency Toolkit for Meeting Planners, Staff, and Attendees

a. First-aid kit which may contain aspirin, Benadryl, Epi-Pen (Note: You cannot administer any drugs. Yet, having these on hand for someone to administer on their own may save a life. Some Meeting Planners do not include any aspirin, Benadryl, or any form of these drugs because there could be consequences.)

b. Flashlights

c. Batteries

d. Hand sanitizer and moist towelettes

e. Extra cell phone cord / solar charger

f. Duct tape

g. Pens / paper / markers

h. Whistle

i. Cash

j. Water / snacks that could be included or obtained from the Hotel / venue. Obviously, it is impracticable that you put together a kit of food / water for everyone, for every meeting. Use your judgment as to what should be contained in your emergency kits.

k. Share the Emergency Toolkit information with Hotel or venue security and other key staff as necessary for their review to identify other items that may need to be included.

l. For more information for your Emergency Toolkit, please see www.ready.gov.

3. If you need to secure rooms for your group in times of crisis, consider the following process that should be prepared for in advance. Kim McGlinn provides a brilliant idea on automating the method to manage the process for displaced travelers and attendees:

a. Develop a meeting management technology attendee registration invitation that can be sent via email to attendees to register for hotel space that you have secured during the time of crisis. For example, if you are planning a day meeting in a city (without hotel sleeping rooms) and there are many attendees that need a room (due to the crisis), you could use your meeting management technology to create an automated solution for those attendees to reserve a hotel room. This will reduce the chaos and multiple emails to and from displaced attendees. Consider the following process:

i.   Secure sleeping rooms at a local hotel during time of crisis.

ii. Use a meeting management technology template / attendee management invitation that can be sent, via email, to your displaced attendees so that they can "check in" and also reserve a sleeping room.

4. If you need to arrange for evacuations, consider discussing crisis management plan evacuations with your ground transportation company and also securing services from companies such as International SOS (iSOS) or iJET International.

5. Sign up for regular news updates from www.Ready.Gov. Then, you will also have access to the Homeland Security, Federal Emergency Management Agency (FEMA), Transportation Security Administration (TSA), NOAA National Weather Service, and other services. Also check the Centers for Disease Control website to view related travel health information, http://wwwnc.cdc.gov/travel/default.aspx. And, before you leave, check the weather forecast for the event destination, www.weather.com.

6. Review this plan with staff, attendees, and security staff from Hotel or venue,and your organization.

Communications with Attendees

1. When preparing attendee communications, include the following information in the pre-communications memos as well as communicating it verbally during the first session.

    • During crisis management situations, the check-in process is to email: name@organization.com and / or call (xxx) xxx-xxxx. This is important so that we know you are safe and your whereabouts. (Or, use the organization's check-in process.)

- All attendees should locate the nearest emergency exit from their hotel room and meeting rooms.

- In an emergency, attendees should try to gather at the indoor meeting location which is:_____ or the outdoor evacuation location which is:_____.

- If you leave the hotel, other than for group events, please remove your name badge.

- If you need to report an emergency, call 911 immediately. Establish the exact location of the emergency (Hotel or venue, address, room, floor, etc.); give your name and contact information. Follow instructions by emergency personnel. The Meeting Planner should be notified of the emergency right away if possible.

Always follow emergency management personnel instructions.

The following guidelines may be standard operating procedures for the Meeting Planner.

1. Ensure that your Crisis Management Plan and Emergency Toolkit are in order. Printed copies of your Crisis Management Plan should be in your bag and possession at all times. The Crisis Management Team contact information should be available to you in print and electronically.

2. Locate emergency exit doors connected to and near the meeting rooms.

3. Locate indoor and outdoor emergency evacuation sites.

4. Locate shelter area that the Hotel or venue has onsite.

5. Take a walk with onsite staff and identify emergency exits, evacuation sites, and shelter areas.

6. Some Hotels and venues do not have good cell phone service especially in the interior of the property. Check your cell phone service and check all landlines that can be used during the meeting to ensure they are working properly.

7. Share the Crisis Management Plan and Emergency Toolkit information with Hotel or venue security and other key staff as necessary. Important to note: Some of the information in the Crisis Management Plan (e.g. attendee disability information) is considered Personal

Identifiable Information (PII) and needs to remain PRIVATE. Information should only be shared if needed, and whoever has the information must dispose of it properly, safely, and completely after the meeting or event concludes.

Onsite at the Meeting / Event DURING a Crisis

1. Call 911 and alert the Hotel or venue if appropriate. There are some incidents documented below where 911 may not be necessary, e.g. concerns raised by an attendee about their room.

2. Remain calm and help maintain order as your attendees and staff will be seeking a leader to provide them with information and directions, especially before official emergency personnel arrive.

3. You should have access to your Crisis Management Plan and Emergency Toolkit. Identify the attendees who may need assistance before others, e.g. attendees with disabilities.

4. Determine if you need to activate the Crisis Management Team process using key stakeholders from the organization. The Crisis Management Team and the process are defined in this Handbook.

5. Be aware of everything occurring, to the best of your ability, as an Incident Report may need to be written. This is also important because emergency personnel, security, or other people may need to know exactly what happened. During or after the crisis, write up one or more reports as applicable using your organization's form or a form similar to what is listed in Appendix C.

6. Listen for instructions for emergency personnel and / or Hotel or venue staff.

7. Assess the situation to the best of your ability and identify next steps.

8. Be prepared to communicate the current state of the environment and attendees to Hotel or venue, or emergency personnel.

9. Begin organizing your Control Room. Think about:

   a. **People**

      i. Who is here (attendees, staff)?

      ii. Who is missing?

      iii. Do I need attendees and staff to begin a check-in process?

      iv. Do I need to contact the organization's home office Security Team?

   b. **Processes**

      i. What process should I follow?

      ii. Are there policies or guidelines in place?

      iii. What reports do I need?

      iv. What reports do I have?

      v. What do I need in hard copy?

      vi. What reports do I need to begin creating?

      vii. What incidents should I track?

      viii. What other resources do I need? (e.g. money, website, weather information, news, etc.)

      ix. What resources do I have?

      x. Reports may include: emergency contact report, attendee report, rooming list, arrival and departure manifests in alphabetic order and in date and time order, attendees who drove to meeting report, special needs reports, and the information that is in the Appendices of this Handbook.

c. **Technology**

    i. Do I have the right equipment?

    ii. Computers?

    iii. Cell phones?

    iv. Flashlights?

    v. Is there a Public Announcement system in place?

10. Notify the organization's home office / Security Team of the emergency and offer frequent updates on the situation and action steps taken.

11. Maintain a written record the crisis and the emergency personnel involved. Include any directives given by key staff such as Hotel or venue staff, emergency staff, security, or others.

12. It may be necessary to consider early departures or evacuation. (See separate section on evacuations in this Handbook.)

    i. Hotel security should check the guest rooms to be sure that attendees are not sleeping or ill. If no one is in the room, the security should put a note on the door indicating where the attendee should go and who to contact.

    ii. If you need to arrange for evacuations, consider discussing crisis management plan evacuations with your ground transportation company and also securing services from companies such as International SOS (iSOS) or iJET International.

13. It may be necessary to consider securing hotel space. Kim McGlinn provides a brilliant idea on automating the method to manage the process for displaced travelers and attendees:

    d. Develop a meeting management technology attendee

registration template that can be sent via email to attendees to register for hotel space that you have secured during the time of crisis. For example, if you are planning a day meeting in a city (without hotel sleeping rooms), and all of a sudden a crisis occurs that requires the attendees to stay in your location, you may want to consider the following process:

iii. Secure sleeping rooms at a local hotel.

iv. Use a meeting management technology template / attendee management module that can be sent, via email, to your displaced attendees so that they can "check in" and also reserve a sleeping room.

v. If you do not use meeting management technology, then use a spreadsheet or paper to begin making a list of the names of people and the nights the rooms are needed.

14. If an attendee needs to go to a medical facility, the Meeting Planner should not transport the attendee in his or her car, but could consider another form of ground transportation if an ambulance is not warranted. If an attendee is taken via ambulance to a hospital or medical clinic, the onsite meeting planner or organization representative should travel with the attendee. Once the attendee is under the care of professional emergency / medical staff the Meeting Planner or other onsite staff may want to stay for a while to ensure that the attendee is under the proper care.

15. Work with the organization's communications, Security Team, or Human Resource team to develop an official communication plan that can be used internally with families. Public announcements or press inquiries should be handled by official organizational communications staff, not Meeting Planners.

Evacuation

It may be necessary to evacuate the Hotel or venue. Typically, this will be an instruction that comes from the Hotel, venue, or emergency personnel.

During the preparation, the Meeting Planner communicated where attendees and staff should meet. It is to be hoped that the predetermined evacuation area is available in this specific crisis event. If an predetermined evacuation area has not been identified, then attendees should go to anywhere that is safe and begin a check-in process as described in this Handbook. During the check-in process, the Meeting Planner can provide more information on where to reconvene if that is the plan. Remember that it may not be safe to use elevators or escalators.

It is not advisable for a Meeting Planner to wait for others to evacuate. Move quickly.

Meeting Planner activities:

1. Bring Crisis Management Plan and the Emergency Toolkits if it is safe to do so.

2. Assist disabled attendees and those with special needs.

3. Identify where the Control Room or area will be established.

4. Begin collecting names of attendees so that a complete roll call can documented. Be sure to report injuries and unaccounted-for attendees or staff to emergency personnel It is important for the Meeting Planner to maintain the roll call list on an ongoing basis. One person should maintain the Control Room desk, yet it may be helpful to have another person go to the other exits to search for attendees, but only if emergency personnel

allow this, or before they arrive. Of course, this would only be advisable if the area is safe.

5. Establish a process for communications with attendees, emergency personnel, and the organization's headquarters.

6. Enter the building ONLY after emergency personnel say it is safe to do so.

Crisis Management Team

The role of the Crisis Management Team is to be responsible for the day-to-day management of crisis incidents. Often the Security Team leader is the person who may brief the organization's leadership team on developments. The Crisis Management Team should include key stakeholders from various departments throughout the organization as well as key suppliers.

The Meeting Planner may notify one or more of the key contacts listed below to begin the Crisis Management Team process. A best practice is for the Meeting Planner to contact one of the members of the Crisis Management Team and then the team can begin contacting others and activate a dial-in conference call bridge for everyone to congregate to discuss next steps.

It is also a best practice to inform managers to contact their direct reports if more resources are necessary.

Crisis Management Team			
Resource	Cell phone	Main phone	Email
Meeting Planning Leader			
Travel Leader			
Operations / Finance Leader (to oversee processes, secure funds)			
Security Leader			
H.R. Leader / Ethics Liaison			
Legal / Compliance Leader			
Communications Leader			

Crisis Management Team			
Resource	Cell phone	Main phone	Email
Information Technology			
Real Estate Leader			
Clergy			
Suppliers: Hotel Ground Offsites			
Others			

Crisis Management Team Process

1. Mobilize the Crisis Management Team; provide a recurring Crisis Management conference call number that can be used during this crisis as well as other crises. Begin the conference call at a designated time and notify the Crisis Management Team, the Meeting Planner(s), the meeting budget holder / requester, the Hotel or venue staff, and other key stakeholders so that they may join the call. See Appendix D for a list of the roles that may need to be on the Crisis Management Team call.

2. One or more people should be responsible for maintaining a journal of all activities, contact information, website addresses and other external intelligence, decisions made, and information that is relevant to the crisis.

3. Meeting Leaders should access their meeting management technology system to identify current and future meetings and attendees that may be affected by this crisis, and who else may need to join this Crisis Management Team call. Determine the plan of action for the other meetings.

4. The Crisis Management Team may create a special mail group for all those affected by the crisis so that email communication may be sent consistently to all those affected.

5. Capture the decisions made by onsite staff, the Crisis Management Team, the Hotel or venue, emergency personnel, etc., so that all information can be provided to the organization and other officials as needed.

    •   Reports should be obtained, reviewed, updated, and

distributed as necessary. Remember that Personal Identifiable Information (PII) may reside in the reports so distribute reports only to those people who need them, and inform them that the information must be disposed of properly as soon as the crisis is over.

6. If hotel space is needed in addition to what the Meeting Planner may secure (or if the Meeting Planner is not in a position to secure hotel space), the Travel Leader or designated person will block space through the Travel Management Company and / or through the Global Sales Organization of the hotel chains.

   • Sample email: "(Organization) is in need of hotel rooms due to the XXX crisis in the (city) area. Please let me know how many rooms you can reserve at our preferred hotels in the (city) area for XX nights beginning immediately. We may need these rooms for up to XX nights. Please call me or email me ASAP the hotels' names, addresses, phone numbers, and number of rooms available for the entire (city) area. Thanks, Travel Leader.

   • The individual properties that are not part of a chain should be contacted as well to determine availability.

   • A point person may be used for impacted travelers and meeting attendees to reach out to. Another method is to set up a registration website through the meeting management technology, and send email invitations to all those travelers and meeting attendees affected. When they "register" they will in turn be assigned one of the available rooms.

7. The meeting planner or another Crisis Management Team member should monitor news broadcasts and research emergency websites. This information should be shared during the ongoing Crisis Management Team calls.

8. If necessary, contact the hospitals closest to the Hotel or venue for assistance in providing medical attention, or locating any missing staff or attendees.

9. If attendees need to be relocated, the Meeting Planner onsite or someone at the organization should begin securing facilities. It may also be an agency such as Red Cross that takes on securing facilities. In addition, transportation to those facilities may be needed as well as a method to identify who and how many attendees need to be transferred.

    *   The person who is responsible for relocation may have to monitor airport conditions, flight changes, communications to and from attendees, and sometimes, communications from attendees' families. Be prepared to document all communications.

10. If the meeting has not started and needs to be cancelled, or the attendees need to leave early, the Meeting Planner and Crisis Management Team need to prepare plans and communicate with:

    *   Attendees and staff

    *   Hotel or venue

    *   Other suppliers (ground transportation, activities, etc.)

11. Develop or activate a method for attendees to "check-in" to confirm they are fine or that they need assistance. Many organizations have automated systems to manage this process today; however, if not, a telephone and email process may be used. Note that it may not be wise to use private social media groups (e.g. a private Facebook group) because those in need may not feel comfortable posting their concerns on Facebook or another social media site. A memo such as the following could be sent to all affected attendees and phone calls could be made to their cell phones:

- Following the (crisis name), (Organization) wants to account for all of our attendees at the (meeting name) as soon as possible. We ask each of you to contact us as soon as possible by either of the following methods:

  i. **Email:** Send an email to (checkin@organization. com) . Please let us know if you are okay or if you need any assistance. Also, if you are with other attendees, please add their names to the email as well. You will get an automatic response message confirming that your email was received.

  ii. **Phone:** Dial the (Organization) emergency hotline at 555-555-5555 (or XXX-XXX-XXXX from outside the U.S.) and report your status. If you are with other attendees, please tell the operator who takes your call the names of those attendees as well. Note, due to heavy call volume, you may be placed on hold for some time before an operator can access your call. You may also experience busy signals when dialing. Please be patient. We urge you to keep trying until you get through.

12. No one should provide information to any outsiders (family, media, etc.) until an approved, written message has been crafted and approved by the organization's official communications or other team. Determine if calls to the attendee's and onsite staff's emergency contacts / families are necessary and what information may be released.

13. If there is limited or loss of communication with the Crisis Management Team, then the onsite Meeting Planner will have to manage using these plans, the closest news affiliate, and prepared communications as sampled in this Handbook.

Emergency Procedures
(alphabetical by emergency type):

In the following pages, a few of the common emergencies and crises are highlighted with guidelines on how to handle them. However, this is not a complete list and the "Types of Crisis" list should be reviewed for a more comprehensive list.

Active Shooter Attack[2]

If a gunman is outside your building:

1. Proceed to a room that can be locked, shut off lights and computer monitors, lock all doors and windows and stay out of sight.

2. Silence cell phones.

3. Take cover under anything available (tables, desks, etc.).

4. One person in the room should call 911.

5. If shots are heard, do not go to investigate their source.

6. Do not leave until given instructions to do so by a uniformed police officer.

RUN – HIDE – FIGHT in that order

1. FEMA recommends evacuation as a first choice, hiding out as a second choice. If the room can be locked, follow the same procedures listed above.

2. If your room cannot be locked, determine if there is a nearby location that can be reached safely and secured or, if you can, safely exit the building. If the room cannot be locked and it is not safe to leave, barricade the door using furniture or anything else that is available.

---

2   Homeland Security and Carnegie Mellon University: Emergency Response Guide

If a gunman enters your office or classroom:

1. Dial 911 if possible and give your location. If you cannot speak, leave the line open so the police can listen to what is taking place.

2. Only as a last resort should you attempt to overpower the shooter with force.

3. If shooting begins, play dead. This may fool the gunman into thinking you are already a victim.

4. If the shooter leaves the area, lock the door and call 911 to provide information to the police. If it is not possible to lock the door, consider relocating to a safe area ONLY if you can do so safely.

After the environment is safe, prepare for the Control Room procedures as well as the Crisis Management Team process, which includes conducting a roll call of attendees and staff; begin the check-in procedure. Journal all of the information as applicable.

Attendee Concerns and Demands

Meeting planners are often faced with attendees who are unhappy or disruptive about the agenda, their room, their roommate, or other situation. It is important that the Meeting Planner handle these concerns professionally.

1. Meeting Planner should obtain the facts of the situation from the individual and begin journaling the information. This should be done in a suitably private setting and information obtained should be maintained confidentially.

2. Meeting Planner should explain the realities of the situation in a suitably private setting (e.g., what the organization's policy is on the situation and how the decisions are made).

3. If the individual is still demanding some action, you may want to ask an onsite senior leader to become involved to talk with the individual. If the concern or demand is escalated, the incident may need to be communicated to the Human Resource representative or Ethics liaison as applicable.

Bomb Threat[3]

1. If the threat is made via telephone, remain calm, and get as much information as possible. Assume the threat is real.

2. If safe to do so, keep the caller on the line and write down everything that is said such as when will it explode, where is the bomb, what does it look like, what will cause it to explode, did you place the bomb, name, race, age, and number from where the call originated. Begin journaling the information.

3. Call 911 immediately and then either you, or someone else, can immediately notify the building, Hotel or venue security.

4. Some bombs may be triggered by cell phones, or other wireless devices so it may be best not to use these devices and use landlines instead.

Bomb or Explosion Actions

1. Get under a sturdy table or desk if things are falling around you. When they stop falling, leave quickly, watching for obviously weakened floors and stairways. As you exit from the building, be especially watchful of falling debris.

2. Leave the building as quickly as possible. Crawl low if there is smoke. Do not stop to retrieve personal possessions or make phone calls.

3. Do not use elevators.

4. Check for fire and other hazards.

5. Once you are out, do not stand in front of windows, glass doors, or other potentially hazardous areas.

6. Move away from sidewalks or streets to be used by emergency officials or others still exiting the building.

7. If you are trapped in debris, use a flashlight, if possible, to signal your location to rescuers.

8. Tap on a pipe or wall so rescuers can hear where you are.

9. If possible, use a whistle to signal rescuers.

---

3   U.S. Government "Emergency Response Plan" http://www.ready.gov

10. Shout only as a last resort. Shouting can cause a person to inhale dangerous amounts of dust.

11. Avoid unnecessary movement so you don't kick up dust.

12. Assist people who are injured, or have special needs or disabilities.

13. Cover your nose and mouth with anything you have on hand. (Dense-weave cotton material can act as a good filter. Try to breathe through the material.)

14. Prepare for the Control Room procedures as well as the Crisis Management Team process, which includes conducting a roll call of attendees and staff; begin the check-in procedure. Journal all of the information as applicable.

Building or Other Construction Collapse

Collapse of a building, an event tent, a stage, or any type of construction is dangerous.

General Guidelines

1. Call 911 and contact the Hotel / venue security.

2. Keep attendees / staff away from the area.

3. Assist people who are injured, or have special needs or disabilities.

4. Follow emergency personnel directions.

5. Report to the predetermined evacuation area and prepare for the Control Room procedures as well as the Crisis Management Team process, which includes conducting a roll call of attendees and staff; begin the check-in procedure. Journal all of the information as applicable.

Crime (Theft of Property, Assault, Other)

Based on the severity of the crime, attendees may or may not want to pursue legal action. Yet, the meeting planner should always contact the organization's and Hotel or venue's security staff to report the incident.

If at a Hotel or venue:

1. Immediately contact Hotel security and, depending upon the nature of the crime, the local authorities (this may be done by the Hotel or the meeting planner) which may be through the 911 system.

2. If the crime involves harm to an attendee, guest, or assets (e.g. laptop), the onsite contact or Meeting Planner should notify the organization's Security Team who will provide you with additional guidance.

3. Journal all of the information.

4. Depending on the severity of the crime, seek medical attention following other procedures documented in this Handbook.

5. If the crime involved theft of the individual's laptop, hotel security and local authorities should be involved. A local police report, in the jurisdiction where the theft occurred, should be filed. Remind the individual to contact their Headquarters office IT representative and Headquarters office HR representative within 24 hours of the theft. They must provide IT with a copy of the police report.

6. The Meeting Planner should notify the meeting sponsor, other Meeting Planners, and others as necessary.

7. If confidential information may have been breached, follow instructions of the organization's Security Team or IT professionals.

8. The individual involved is responsible for his / her property and for any follow-up with the Hotel and his / her insurance company. Usually, the organization will not reimburse individuals for the loss of personal assets per policies.

9. The Meeting Planner should be sympathetic to the situation but is not responsible for on-going involvement once he or she has put the individual in touch with the Hotel or venue, local authorities, and / or if applicable, the organization's

Security Team. The Meeting Planner should inform the individual that if, after an appropriate period of time, the individual believes that the Hotel's response has not been adequate, the individual can contact the organization's Security Team for further assistance.

Death of a Participant

1. If at a Hotel or venue, the Meeting Planner should call 911 and the Hotel or venue staff.

2. Emergency personnel are equipped to manage the body, yet it is extremely important to know the right process to notify the emergency contacts.

3. Clergy may need to be called.

4. Journal all of the information.

5. If it is the organization's employee, the Meeting Planner should call the organization's Headquarters office Human Resource contact immediately and provide emergency contact information. The Headquarters office Human Resource staff should contact appropriate management to determine who is best positioned to reach out and talk to the emergency contact / family. The individual's Headquarters office Human Resource contact is responsible for involving / informing relevant department team members as applicable.

6. If it is an external attendee such as a client, the Meeting Planner should contact the meeting sponsor's organization's Headquarters office Security contact immediately, and the applicable leader should contact the emergency contact.

7. The Meeting Planner should immediate notify the organization's Security Team, the meeting sponsor, and other leadership as applicable.

8. It may be necessary to communicate with other attendees that the loss was unfortunate and that the organization took significant efforts in managing the loss with the family, without going into detail.

Earthquake[4]

Stay as safe as possible during an earthquake. Be aware that some earthquakes are actually foreshocks and a larger earthquake might occur. Minimize your movements to a few steps to a nearby safe place and stay indoors until the shaking has stopped and you are sure exiting is safe.

If Indoors:

1. Drop to the ground; take cover by getting under a sturdy table or other piece of furniture; cover your face, and wait until the shaking stops. If there isn't a table or desk near you, cover your face and head with your arms and crouch in an inside corner of the building.

2. Stay away from glass, windows, outside doors and walls, and anything that could fall.

3. Stay in bed if you are there when the earthquake strikes. Protect your head with a pillow.

4. Use a doorway for shelter only if it is in close proximity to you and if you know it is a strongly supported, load-bearing doorway.

5. Stay inside until shaking stops and it is safe to go outside. Research has shown that most injuries occur when people inside buildings attempt to move to a different location inside the building or try to leave.

6. Be aware that the electricity may go out or the sprinkler systems or fire alarms may turn on.

7. Do not use the elevators.

If Outdoors:

1. Stay there.

2. Move away from buildings, streetlights, and utility wires.

3. Once in the open, stay there until the shaking stops. The

---

4   Federal Emergency Management Agency (FEMA), "Are You Ready?" pg. 97-99

greatest danger exists directly outside buildings, at exits, and alongside exterior walls. Ground movement during an earthquake is seldom the direct cause of death or injury. Most earthquake-related casualties result from collapsing walls, flying glass, and falling objects.

After Shaking Stops:

1. Listen for instructions via the PA system, Hotel/venue Security or emergency personnel.

2. Do not leave the facility unless instructed to do so. If outdoors, do not re-enter the facility unless instructed to do so.

3. Report to Control Room or predetermined evacuation area.

4. Do not use regular or cellular phones except to report emergencies.

5. Assist people who are injured, or have special needs or disabilities.

6. Be prepared for aftershocks.

7. Journal all of the information as applicable.

What are the biggest dangers?

1. Falling objects (pictures, items in cupboards and on shelves, fixtures, furniture, file cabinets, and book shelves).

2. Swinging doors and broken windows.

3. Building collapse.

4. Fires (from broken natural gas lines or electrical).

After an earthquake:

If safe, report to the predetermined evacuation area and prepare for the Control Room procedures as well as the Crisis Management Team process, which includes conducting a roll call of attendees and staff; begin the check-in procedure.

Fire

Call 911 at the first indication of a fire and then call the Hotel or venue contacts.

1. Evacuate the area immediately. When the smoke alarm sounds, or even if it doesn't, get out fast. Move safely away and direct attendees away from fire and smoke to the designated evacuation area. Assist people who have special needs or disabilities.

2. If you are traveling in the stairwell[5] and you starting noticing smoke in the lower stairwells, it is a sign that there is denser smoke further down. Do not continue down the stairs. Turn around immediately and climb back up, all the way to the roof. Once on the roof, prop the door wide open. It will draw air up the stairwell, helping to clear the smoke gathered at the bottom. This is the only door you should leave open when moving through a building on fire. Move to the side of the roof from which the wind is coming and remain there until help comes.

3. Take emergency kits with you if it is safe to do so. Do not stand upright, but crawl or keep low to the floor to avoid smoke and odorless carbon monoxide. Before opening any door, check the temperature of the door with the back of your hand. If a door is hot, DO NOT OPEN IT. Go to the nearest exit, closing doors between you and the fire.

   a. If you cannot leave your room (or the meeting room) signal to emergency personnel by hanging extra clothes, a bed sheet, or something from the window. If there is smoke in your room, open the window. Do not break the glass unless it is absolutely necessary because heavier smoke may begin to enter from outside. If you are in your sleeping room, fill the bathtub with water. Wet towels and sheets and stuff them around the door

---

5   Travel Responsibly, Informed, and Protected (TRIP); http://trip.ustia.org/safety/tips/1173/how-to-escape-during-a-hotel-fire/

and vents which are allowing smoke to enter the room. If the door and walls are hot, bail water on them with your ice bucket to keep them cool. Place the mattress[6] up against the door and hold it in place with the dresser. Keep everything as wet as possible. If there is a fire outside of the window, pull down the drapes and move everything that is flammable away from the window. Do not jump from the room. A fall from most heights can cause serious injury. Rather, continue to protect yourself from the fire and signal from your window for help.

4. Direct emergency personnel and / or Hotel security to the emergency.

5. Listen for and follow the emergency personnel directions.

6. If clothes catch fire, stop, drop, and roll – stop immediately, drop to the ground, and cover your face with your hands. Roll over and over or back and forth until the fire is out. If you or someone else cannot stop, drop, and roll, smother the flames with a blanket or towel. Use cool water to treat the burn immediately for 3 to 5 minutes. Cover with a clean, dry cloth.

7. If it is not safe to enter the building, meet at the designated evacuation area for further instruction.

8. Report to the predetermined evacuation area and prepare for the Control Room procedures as well as the Crisis Management Team process, which includes conducting a roll call of attendees and staff; begin the check-in procedure.

9. Journal all of the information as applicable.

Flood

Call 911 at the first indication of a fire and then call the Hotel or venue contacts.

---

6   Travel Responsibly, Informed, and Protected (TRIP); http://trip.ustia.org/safety/tips/1172/what-to-do-if-trapped-inside-your-room-during-a-hotel-fire/

Floods may result in drowning, accidents, and electrocution.

General Flood Guidelines

1. Stay away from anything electrical. You may turn off anything electrical but only if it isn't wet and you are not standing in water. Otherwise, do not touch anything electrical.

2. If it is safe to do so, wait for emergency personnel to arrive. Direct them to the emergency.

3. Move safely away and direct attendees away from flood to the designated evacuation area that is on higher ground. Assist people who have special needs or disabilities. If water rises before you evacuate, go to the top floor or roof.

4. Do not attempt to walk across flooded areas.

5. Listen to a battery-operated radio for the latest storm information.

6. Use hand sanitizer or soap and water to cleanse body, hands, or other areas that have come in contact with flood waters.

7. Report to the predetermined evacuation area and prepare for the control room procedures as well as the Crisis Management Team process, which includes conducting a roll call of attendees and staff; begin the check-in procedure.

8. Journal all of the information as applicable.

Hurricane

Hurricane hazards may be titled tropical depression, tropical storm, or hurricane, and may cause floods.

1. Monitor hurricane situation by using local and national news, and the National Hurricane Center for information http://www.nhc.noaa.gov/ .

2. Along with information from your Crisis Management Team, the National Hurricane Center, and other officials, a decision must be made on whether you and the attendees will evacuate or stay at the Hotel or venue.

3. If you plan to evacuate, then it is time to put in place the Crisis Management Plans that you discussed before your meeting with your Travel Management Company and your ground transportation supplier. In addition, if you have emergency support providers such as iSOS or iJet, then contact them for assistance.

4. If you are staying at the Hotel or venue, then it is time to discuss what activities will cease and provide ongoing regular communications to the attendees. If staying at the Hotel or venue, the Security Team may want to assemble attendees into a location that the property officials suggest, and that does not contain windows or glass exposed to the exterior walls and windows.

5. Start the Crisis Management Team process, which includes conducting a roll call of attendees and staff; maintain the check-in procedure before, during, and after the hurricane. Attendees may need to report their whereabouts and safety to family and others.

6. Assist people who are injured, or have special needs or disabilities.

7. Journal all of the information as applicable.

Illness of One or More Attendees / Staff

Sometimes an attendee or staff member has an illness that requires an early departure but may not warrant a hospital visit.

1. The Meeting Planner should assist attendee with arranging airline flights, arranging ground transportation to the airport, and checking out of the hotel.

2. The Meeting Planner should provide comfort to the attendee if welcomed and considered warranted in the circumstances. This may involve accompanying him / her to the airport or, within reason, to their destination. It is acceptable for the onsite contact or Meeting Planner to transport to the individual to the airport but, as mentioned

earlier, not to the hospital. The Meeting Planner or staff member may transport an attendee as long as the attendee is not severely ill or injured. In those circumstances, an alternative form of transportation should be arranged.

3. The Meeting Planner should inquire of the attendee if there are any individuals to be contacted, and follow up as requested.

4. The Meeting Planner should inform speaker / instructor / facilitator of the attendee's early departure and keep details confidential.

5. Journal all of the information as applicable.

6. Any incremental costs of the early departure may be charged to the organization or to the attendee (if is an external attendee who paid for his / her own travel arrangements), as determined by policy or practice.

Inappropriate Behavior (including behavior related to excessive alcohol or drug intake)

1. If a Meeting Planner witnesses the situation first hand and feels comfortable in dealing with it directly, he / she should approach the individual and advise him / her to stop the behavior – remind him / her of their professional responsibilities. Alternatively, the Meeting Planner should contact a senior onsite representative who will address the situation.

2. Journal all of the information as applicable.

3. If the behavior continues and is disruptive, offensive, or puts the individual or others at physical risk, contact Hotel or venue security and ask them to intervene. The Meeting Planner may accompany Hotel or venue security to monitor how incident is handled, in accordance with security protocols.

4. If the behavior results in injury, follow the guidelines in this Handbook.

5. Once the immediate situation has been handled, the

Meeting Planner should engage the meeting sponsor or senior onsite representative to discuss any further action to be taken.

6. The Meeting Planner, onsite representative, or meeting sponsor may want to consult with the organization's Security Team, Ethics liaison, or Human Resources to consider actions to be taken.

7. Depending on the severity of the behavior, the meeting sponsor, Security Team, Ethics or Human Resources representative should decide whether the participant should be sent home and if other leaders need to be notified.

8. The facts of an incident and any resulting conversations should be documented and, if appropriate, provided to the Security Team, Human Resources, or the Ethics liaison regardless if it is an organization attendee, staff, or external attendee. If the Hotel or venue security becomes involved, obtain a copy of their report and inform the organization's Security Team who will provide additional guidance if appropriate.

9. If the information is brought to the Meeting Planner after the fact, even if still onsite, the Meeting Planner should reach out to the organization's Security Team, Ethics liaison or Human Resources representative who will recommend next steps and may ultimately take on-going responsibility for actions to be taken.

10. If you believe that an individual may seek to drive under the influence of alcohol or drugs, suggest that the individual not drive and ask for keys or suggest that he / she take a taxi or spend the night in a hotel. Ask a more senior individual onsite to talk to the individual under the influence. Document the conversation, no additional action should be taken. Depending on the severity, the Meeting Planner may refer to the organization's Security Team, Human Resource representative, or Ethics leader for follow-up the next day. If an individual under the influence becomes sick, follow the guidance in this Handbook.

11. If another attendee complains about another individual's behavior, the Meeting Planner should obtain the facts of the situation from both individuals. This should be done in a suitably private setting and information obtained should be maintained confidentially and communicated to the appropriate Security Team, Ethics liaison, or Human Resource representative. The onsite contact or Meeting Planner should, on behalf of the attendee, contact the Security Team, Ethics liaison, or Human Resources representative. Once informed, the representative will handle the situation and provide the Meeting Planner with guidance on any next steps they should take.

Incarceration

When an attendee or staff member at your meeting is incarcerated, the following steps should be followed:

1. The Meeting Planner should obtain the facts from all available resources and contact the organization's Security Team immediately for next steps.

2. Journal all of the information as applicable.

3. The Security Team may need to contact the Legal Department or other resources such as Human Resources.

4. The Meeting Planner or others representing the organization should normally not bail out the attendee unless the Security Team agrees it is the best way forward.

5. The Meeting Planner may make calls on behalf of the attendee if the attendee requests such actions.

6. Information must remain private and should not be shared among others at the meeting or with others in the organization.

Information Security Breach

Information Security Breaches may occur on the following, but are not limited to:

- Computers / laptops
- Electronic storage devices (e.g. USB / flash drives, CDs, DVDs, etc.)
- Email (e.g. sent unsecured to an unauthorized recipient, hacked email, etc.)
- Electronic documents (e.g. access to unsecured computer by unauthorized individual, failure to destroy files, etc.)
- Paper documents (e.g. loss, unauthorized duplication or theft, failure to destroy hard copy as required, etc.)

The organization most likely has a standard operating procedure for the collection, storage, sharing, and destruction of data. In addition, it most likely has a process that must be followed to report a breach of security. The Meeting Planner is to follow those processes.

The best thing to do is to have the contacts of the Security Team and IT team handy, as well as any checklists they may provide to you, to maintain information properly.

For example, some organizations use shredders onsite at meetings. If this is normal protocol, then documents cannot be left in the meeting room after the meeting concludes. Those documents either need to be returned to the organization or shredded based on the protocols.

Name of Security and IT Staff (or other leader responsible for technology security breaches)	Email Address	Work Phone	Work Cell	Personal Cell	Home Phone

Medical Emergencies[7]

Always report a medical emergency.

If the Meeting Planner is not aware, and the attendee notifies the Hotel or venue:

- Inform the Hotel that if an incident is critical and occurs in the middle of the night, the Meeting Planner should be notified immediately. Obtain a copy of the Security report.

- If the incident is not critical, the Hotel or venue need not awaken the Meeting Planner but should notify the planner first thing in the morning. The Meeting Planner should immediately follow up with the attendee. Obtain a copy of the Security Report.

Critical Steps to Follow

1. If critical, call 911 and contact the Hotel or venue staff to ensure they are informed of the situation. Let the 911 dispatcher lead the call and follow instructions provided by the dispatcher.

2. DO NOT hang up until dispatcher tells you to.

3. Provide emergency personnel with the information they request (e.g. nature of injury, hazards involved, nearest entrance or access point to person).

4. Remain calm and assess the situation, surroundings, and potential hazards before approaching the injured person.

5. Do not move the injured person unless they are in danger of further injury.

6. Take precautions to prevent contact with body fluids and exposure to bloodborne pathogens.

7. Meeting Planners, or others nearby, who are trained in CPR or First Aid and who want to / feel comfortable stepping forward to provide these services, may do so until other emergency personnel arrive.

---

7   Some of the data is from the Emergency Response Plan, Ready.gov/business

8. If it is safe to do so, wait at the location for emergency personnel to arrive. Ask someone near you to direct the emergency personnel to your location as soon as they arrive. If safe, stay until emergency personnel no longer need your assistance or further information.

9. If the attendee needs to leave the facility to seek further medical attention, the Meeting Planner or other onsite staff should accompany and remain with him / her unless otherwise instructed by the organization's Security Team or other staff.

10. If the attendee can respond, ask him / her who they want contacted (personal and professional). The organization's Security Team contact or Human Resource contact is responsible for contacting the attendee's emergency contact.

11. Journal all of the information as applicable.

Missing Person

1. Contact 911

2. Journal all of the information received (e.g. last time person was seen, information from witnesses, what the person may have been wearing, what the person may have with missing person, last person who talked with the missing person, etc.).

3. Do not go into the hotel room; only officials should have access to hotel room because there may be evidence in the room.

4. Contact the organization's Security Team or Human Resource contact immediately. Allow them to contact the missing person's family. They will also determine the best way to handle the media.

Pandemic

General precautions[8] can greatly reduce the risk of exposure to infectious agents. Yet, it is the responsibility of

---

8   World Health Organization (WHO)
     http://www.who.int/ith/other_health_risks/infectious_diseases/en/index.html

the Meeting Planner and the organization's Security Team to inform attendees of any particular hazards to personal safety and security presented by the destination.

Information can be found on the Centers for Disease Control (CDC) website: http://wwwn.cdc.gov/travel/destinationList.aspx.

If a pandemic occurs, it is important to coordinate activities while maintaining safety.

1. Identify local hospitals and available emergency personnel who can provide assistance.

2. Determine how to quarantine people as necessary with the Hotel or venue if the attendee(s) is not going to a hospital.

3. Determine the best way to cleanse and disinfect. The CDC has recommendations for cleaning flu, MRSA, water-related emergencies, body fluid spills, rodents, etc. There are far too many to list in this Handbook, but generally, it is important to use stringent hand-hygiene products, soap, detergents, and ensure that all waste is properly disposed of so it does not come in contact with people.

4. Obtain and distribute information about personal protection and response strategies with other attendees (e.g. hand washing, use of hand gels, cough/sneeze etiquette, emergency contingency plans, travel policies).

5. Work directly with the organization's Security Team. It may be necessary for the Security Team or other leaders to execute controls such as isolating affected travelers, restricting travel, etc.

6. Journal all of the information as applicable.

Power Outage

Most Meeting Planners have experienced some form of a black-out. Hopefully, the power outage is short-term vs. long-term. A power outage may occur with or without downed power lines. Be careful if you are unsure of the obstacles that may be in your path. Stay away from downed power lines and report them.

Your emergency kit should provide you with many of the items needed during a power outage.

1. Notify the Hotel or venue immediately. If it is an emergency situation (e.g. injuries, sparks, wide-spread, etc.) it may warrant a call to 911.

2. If an evacuation is necessary, report to the predetermined evacuation area and prepare for the control room procedures as well as the Crisis Management Team process, which includes conducting a roll call of attendees and staff; begin the check-in procedure.

3. Journal all of the information as applicable.

Protests / Disturbances

A civil protest[9] will usually take the form of an organized public demonstration of disapproval or display disagreement with an idea or course of action. It should be noted that in *many* cases protests such as marches, meetings, picketing, and rallies will be peaceful and non-obstructive. However, a disturbance may also be informal and be between two people.

1. Call 911 if necessary and alert Hotel or venue staff.

2. Ask all attendees and staff to remove name badges.

3. If it is safe to do so, wait for emergency personnel. If not, evacuate.

4. Evacuation may not be possible if the protestors have used common tactics such as blocking streets and entrances, setting fires in the street, chaining themselves to objects to make it difficult to arrest them, locking arms, erecting

---

9   Planning and Managing Security for Major Special Events, http://www.cops.usdoj.gov/Publications/e07071299_web.pdf

platforms and stages, etc. If this is the case, it is best to remain in the location and lock the doors and windows.

5. Direct attendees away from the disturbance or protest and if you are outside, return to the Hotel or venue immediately.

6. Do not attempt to get involved in a disturbance and instruct attendees to stay clear of presenting positions or getting involved.

7. Notify the Crisis Management Team or organization's Security Team immediately.

8. Journal all of the information as applicable.

Suicide

Should an attendee *commit* suicide - see section titled "Death" for action steps.

Should an attendee *attempt* to commit suicide and death does not occur - see action steps below.

1. All comments heard or reported which seriously suggest the possibility of someone taking his or her own life must be taken very seriously. The first point of contact may be 911 and a senior onsite leader. The emergency personnel will provide additional guidance.

2. If the attendee has injured himself or herself, the Meeting Planner should call 911.

3. Once police and hospital, if appropriate, have been contacted, the Meeting Planner should contact the organization's Security Team who will provide internal guidance surrounding the involvement of Human Resources and contacting the individual's emergency contact(s).

4. Journal all of the information as applicable.

Threats

Threats may be to an attendee, staff, suppliers, or others and it may be to injure or kill.

1. All comments heard should be taken seriously. Capture the date and time of the threat, exactly what was said, how the threat was made, the communication method (e.g. in-person, via phone, via email, etc.), indication as to the reason for the threat, and what the person wants in return (if applicable).

2. Call 911 if necessary and alert Hotel or venue staff.

3. Direct attendees away from the disturbance or protest and if you are outside, return to the Hotel or venue immediately.

4. Do not attempt to get involved in a disturbance and instruct attendees to stay clear of presenting positions or getting involved.

5. Notify the Crisis Management Team or organization's Security Team immediately.

6. Journal all of the information as applicable.

Tornado

Before a tornado[10] hits, the wind may die down and the air may become very still.

A cloud of debris can mark the location of a tornado even if a funnel is not visible. Tornadoes generally occur near the trailing edge of a thunderstorm. It is not

uncommon to see clear, sunlit skies behind a tornado.

What to Do Before a Tornado

1. Be alert to changing weather conditions.

2. Listen to NOAA Weather Radio (www.weather.gov/nwr) or to commercial radio or television newscasts for the latest information.

3. Look for approaching storms, be prepared to take shelter immediately.

4. Look for the following danger signs:

10 FEMA, pg. 58-64.

- Dark, often greenish sky
- Large hail
- A large, dark, low-lying cloud (particularly if rotating)
- Loud roar, similar to a freight train.

What to Do During a Tornado

1. If you are under a tornado warning, seek shelter immediately.

2. An interior[11] room on the lowest level away from corners, windows, doors, and outside walls is most desirable.

3. If you cannot get to the shelter area, or are in your sleeping room, go to the center of an interior room on the lowest level (closet, interior hallway) away from corners, windows, doors, outside walls. Put as many walls as possible between you and the outside. If you are in a Hotel or venue, go to the shelter area and get under a sturdy table. Use your arms to protect your head and neck.

What to Do After a Tornado

Be aware of your surroundings as there may be significant damage.

1. Listen for instructions via the Public Announcement system, the Hotel or venue security, or emergency personnel. Direct emergency personnel to the injured and disabled persons.

2. Do not leave the Hotel or venue unless instructed to do so. If outdoors, do not re-enter the Hotel or venue unless instructed to do so.

3. Be careful when walking to any area that has been damaged. Look for broken glass, downed power lines, flooding, etc.

4. Report to the Control Room (either inside or at the predetermined evacuation area). Prepare for the Control Room procedures as well as the Crisis Management Team process, which includes conducting a roll call of attendees and staff; begin the check-in procedure.

---

11   Federal Emergency Management Association (FEMA), "Are You Ready?" pg. 39

Toxic / Chemical Emergencies

While some toxic chemicals are noticeable, others are odorless. Exposure could cause severe illness or even death.

General Toxic / Chemical Guidelines

1. Call 911 and notify Hotel or venue security. Be prepared to provide the following information:

    • There is a toxic / chemical emergency.

    • The location of the substance.

    • Type of substance or what caused the situation.

    • If there are any injuries.

2. Determine, with emergency personnel and security, if it makes most sense to evacuate the area or stay inside.

    • Outside12 – stay upstream, uphill, and upwind. In general, try to go at least one-half mile (usually 8-10 city blocks) from the danger area. Do not walk into or touch any spilled liquids, airborne mists, or condensed solid chemical deposits.

    • Indoors – If requested to stay indoors, close and lock all exterior doors and windows. Close vents and as many interior doors as possible. Turn off air conditioners and ventilation systems. Go into the pre-selected shelter room. Use materials to fill cracks and holes in room.

3. Assist any injured or disabled people or people with special needs.

4. Do not attempt to clean spills or extinguish flames.

5. Do not smoke or light a match in the vicinity of the toxic spill.

6. Report to the predetermined evacuation area and prepare for the Control Room procedures as well as the Crisis Management Team process, which includes conducting a roll call of attendees and staff; begin the check-in procedure.

---

12 Federal Emergency Management Association (FEMA), "Are You Ready?" pg. 132

My Page of Notes

Appendix A:
Onsite Crisis Management Contact Sheet

Please keep the Contact Sheet in electronic form and hard copy with you at all times.

Meeting Name			
Meeting Planner Contact		Cell Phone	
Meeting Requesters Contact		Cell Phone	
Dates			
Hotel/Venue Name			
Address			
City/State		Main Hotel Phone	
HOTEL/VENUE EMERGENCY INFORMATION			
Police, Fire, Ambulance		CALL 911	
Hotel/Venue Emergency #		CALL Ext #	
Hotel/Venue Non-Emergency Extension		Extension #	
Hotel/Venue Security Director	Director Name here	Cell Phone#	
Evacuation Outdoor Area	Describe Outdoor location here		
Indoor Relocation/Meeting Area	Describe Indoor location here		
Hotel Staff Emergency Command Center	Location here		
Automated External Defibrillators	☐ Yes	☐ No Quantity and Locations:	
CPR Certified Staff	☐ Yes	☐ No Name(s) and Contact Information	
Public Address System	☐ Yes	☐ No	
Doctor on Call	☐ Yes	☐ No Name(s) and Contact information	

HOSPITAL AND PHARMACY			
Nearest Hospital with 24-hr Emergency Services		Nearest 24-hr Pharmacy	
Address		Address	
City, State, Zip		City, State, Zip	
Website		Website	
Phone		Phone	
Directions		Directions	

EMERGENCY CONTACTS		
Staff Office/Control Room	Location	Phone (if any)
Travel Management Company for Transportation	After Hours Emergency	(800) 823-9017
Onsite Lead and Main Emergency Contact	Name	Cell
Onsite Staff	Name	Cell
Note the following after each name:	Name	Cell
C = CPR Certified	Name	Cell

Appendix B:

Important Numbers

TRANSPORTATION (numbers verified 9/12)

Flight Stats: http://www.flightstats.com to track flight status and airport delays.

Travel Management Company 24 / 7 Phone Number: _____

Travel Management Company website: _____

Travel Management Company primary contact and phone number for Group Travel: _____

_____

Airlines	Airlines	Car Rental	Greyhound
Air Canada (888) 247-2262	Porter Airlines (888) 619-8622	Ace (317) 248-5686	214-849-8966 7am-7pm CST M-F
Alaska Air (800)-252-7522	Southwest (800) 435-9792	Alamo (800) 222-9075	www.greyhound. com
Allegiant Air (702) 505-8888	Spirit Air (800) 772-7117	Avis (800) 331-1212	
American (800) 433-7300	Sun Country (800) 359-6786	Budget (800)527-0700	Amtrak
Air Tran (800) 247-8726	United (800) 864-8331	Dollar (800) 800-4000	(800)872-7245
Delta (800) 221-1212	US Airways (800) 428-4322	Enterprise (800) 261-7331	www.amtrak.com
Frontier (800) 432-1359	Virgin America (877) 359-8474	Hertz (800) 654-3131	
Jet Blue (800) 538-2583	WestJet (888) 937-8538	National (877) 222-9058	
		Payless (800) 729-5377	
		Thrifty (800) 847-4389	

HOTEL CHAINS

(Preferred Chain #1)	(Preferred Chain #2)	(Preferred Chain #3)
(Global Sales Rep name)	(Global Sales Rep name)	(Global Sales Rep name)
(Phone Number and Email)	(Phone Number and Email)	(Phone Number and Email)

GROUND TRANSPORTATION

(Ground Transportation Co. #1)	(Ground Transportation Co. #2)	(Ground Transportation Co. #3)
(Contact Name)	(Contact Name)	(Contact Name)
(Phone Number and Email)	(Phone Number and Email)	(Phone Number and Email)

PASSPORTS/VISAS

Universal Passport & Visas	International Visa Service	A Briggs Passport & Visa Expeditors
http://www.upvhq.com/	http://ivsdc.com/	http://www.abriggs.com/
(800) 831-2098	(800) 222-8472	(800) 806-0581

OTHER IMPORTANT CONTACTS

USA Embassy Links www.usembassy.gov

Department of Homeland Security www.dhs.gov

World Health Organization www.who.int

U.S. Centers for Disease Control and Prevention www.cdc.gov   (800) 232-4636

Flu.Gov www.flu.gov

FEMA (800) 621-3362   Click here for FEMA State Office web Links

Red Cross www.redcross.org   1-800-733-2767

WEATHER

National Weather Service	http://www.weather.gov/	The Weather Channel	www.weather.com

NEWS AFFILIATES

ABC	CBS	NBC	CNN
www.abcnews.go.com	www.cbsnews.com	www.nbcnews.com	www.cnn.com

EMERGENCY NUMBERS

Organization's Main Office Number:

Organization's Security Office Number:

Appendix C:
Incident Report

Please complete the Incident Report and add additional pages as necessary. Completed forms should be sent to a member of the Crisis Management Team. If there are police reports or security reports from the Hotel or venue, please attach them as well.

Meeting Information			
Meeting / Event Name			
Name of Person Completing Report		Contact Information for Person Completing Report	Phone: Email:
Description of the Incident: (who, what, when, where, why)			
Date of the Incident:			
Time of the Incident:			
Location of the Incident:			
Witnesses to the Incident (obtain name and contact information)			
Actions taken:			
Follow-up to the Incident:			
Complete Only If This Incident Was Reported to the Police			
Police Station Name, Phone Number:			
Police Station Address:			
Name and Phone Number of Officer in Charge:			

Appendix D:
Sample Communications

Sample Communications #1 - Travel in and out of Boston

(Organization name) is dedicated to caring for our employees during times of crisis. Due to a "XXXXXX" in the Boston area, all flights in and out of Boston's Logan International Airport including all surrounding airports (Worcester Regional Airport) have been canceled until damage assessments have been made by the FAA. All surrounding train stations are closed as well. We assume the airport, as well as the train stations, will be closed for at least XX days.

We have determined that approximately 200 (Organization name) employees including personnel attending local meetings are possibly stranded in the Boston area and with the cancellation of all flights and train stations closed, our rental car company (Name of Supplier) has been contacted and approximately one hundred (100) rentals have been reserved for any employee who wants to consider driving. If bus transportation is needed, we can charter motor coaches and charge a central account.

We have secured 150 rooms for the next XX days to protect our travelers who may have become stranded, and (name of Meeting Planner, the planner onsite), has secured rooms for those participating in the meeting. Travel and Meeting Services have separate American Express cards to which emergency expenses can be charged to lessen the burden on our travelers. The hotel rooms in the Boston area have been charged to this account.

We will continue to monitor all FAA announcements until further notice. When airports open, it will take several days to process all delayed passengers and return to normal flight operations. If any travelers require assistance, please contact our team at the following phone numbers and email addresses:

Name and Title	Office Phone	Cell Phone	Home Phone	Email Address

Sample Communications #2 – Monitoring Situation

(Organization's) Crisis Management and Meetings teams are watching the progress of Hurricane (Name). At this stage, most predictions have the storm crossing the (area) from west to east late in the day on (day / date). Indications are that (city) area will experience tropical storm-force winds and some heavy rains – but not the full impact of the storm. A storm this powerful is highly unpredictable, however, and we will be monitoring it closely over the next 48 hours.

Based on current storm predictions, we are planning to maintain our original starting dates and times for your meeting. Our first concern is for the safety of our meeting attendees, and we will continue to monitor the progress of Hurricane (name) closely. We will post updates on the meeting status to the meeting website. Should the situation change such that we need to alter event plans, we will notify you as early as possible by posting a notice on that site and sending an email directly to you.

To view the status updates, please visit the event website at: INSERT LINK

As with any major storm, Hurricane (name) has the potential to disrupt flight schedules long before and after it passes. We recommend that you visit your airline's website and news sources to stay up-to-date on flight delays and cancellations. Thank you for bearing with us during this period of unpredictability.

Sample Communications #3 – Meeting Postponed

After conferring with (Organization's name) Crisis Management Team, the decision has been made to cancel this week's (Meeting name) in light of the likely impact of Hurricane (name) on (state) and specifically the (city name) area in the next few days. Latest projections suggest a high likelihood that strong winds, tornados, and significant rainfall may impact the (city name) area starting today and running through (day). The impact of Hurricane (name) has been especially difficult to predict; however, the best information and judgment of the experts make it clear that the prudent decision is to defer (Meeting name) to another week.

Your travel arrangements for (Meeting name) will be automatically cancelled. You do not need to do anything further at this time. Please do not contact our (Travel Management Company's Group Travel) directly. If you have any questions regarding (Meeting name) please feel free to contact (name, phone number, email address, and hours of operation).

They will be responding to messages beginning (day) morning at (time) when they reopen.

Preparations are already underway to reschedule (Meeting name) to another date (and potentially a different location), and we will provide more information to you on the rescheduling as it becomes available. Our intent is to reschedule sometime this (year, season, etc.) or early (month) at the latest but availability of a facility that can accommodate this program will be the primary factor impacting when and where we reschedule.

We apologize for the inconvenience the cancellation and subsequent rescheduling of (Meeting name) will cause you. However, your safety is our paramount concern and we are confident that, given the current projections, we have made the right decision.

Appendix E:
Sample Role Play

Even though crisis management documents are helpful to Meeting Planners, the best method for planners to learn how to manage a situation is through full simulation exercises or role plays of crises. Role plays build capability and reveal process gaps. Because each crisis is different, repeated simulations of various sorts of crisis situations will greatly expand and reinforce the ability of attendees to respond well in the moment. Ideally, Meeting Planners, along with other key stakeholders, should enact crisis simulations quarterly or more frequently.

Below we highlight one of the numerous crisis management activities that Debi Scholar has used with clients. During this 90-minute exercise, we assemble a Crisis Management Team and processes. We use a teleconference bridge and a Control Room. When we conduct the role play exercises, Debi adds additional facts at 15-minute intervals throughout the process, such as:

- We learn that there are at least 10 attendees with life-threatening injuries
- We learn that one supplier cannot fulfill our requests
- We learn that information was leaked to the media about one of our attendees

While the following role play is focused on a hurricane situation, other role plays should also be enacted such as spousal attacks with guns, terrorist attacks, toxic chemicals in the air, etc. Contact Debi if you would like your team to experience these role plays to improve your crisis management plans and processes.

Hurricane Role Play with Meeting Planner and Crisis Management Team

Step 1	Mitigation

- Meeting requester wants to conduct Meeting / Event in high risk hurricane location during hurricane season
- Meeting Planner informs meeting requester about the risks of holding a meeting in a known hurricane location during hurricane season, and recommends a different location

Step 2	Preparedness

Meeting Planner and Crisis Management Team enact a 90-minute role play of Hurricane to prepare for the crisis

Time:	Situation:	Role:	Actions Taken
10:00 a.m.	Hurricane approaching	Meeting Planner	Activates Crisis Management Team (or the Crisis Management Team is activated by someone else)
10:05 a.m.	Hurricane approaching		
		Meeting Planner	Provides local information about the situation and the number of attendees onsite
		Travel Contact	Provides information about air travel situation
		Security Contact	Provides information about what the professional sources are estimating for the hurricane. Leads the conference call, may make recommendations based on other information obtained
		H.R. Contact	Provides information about how many other staff may work in the area
		Legal / Compliance Contact	Provides guidance on legal responsibilities
		IT Contact	Provides support such as setting up a mail group; may be asked to pull reports as necessary
		Real Estate Contact	Provides information about local office shelter information if necessary
		Finance Contact	Provides information on how to obtain funding if necessary
		Communications / PR Contact	Crafts the communications that will go to attendees and staff

	Hotel Supplier	Provides detail on whether or not they are expected to evacuate, offers additional rooms if needed in addition to the attendees' rooms
	Ground Transportation Supplier	Offers ground transportation services to office location, airport, or other location
	Rental Car Supplier	Offers rental cars for those people who want to evacuate and drive
11:00 a.m.	Hurricane hits; most attendees did not evacuate; hotel is severely damaged	
	Meeting Planner	Starts the Control Room and Onsite Crisis Management Plan procedures including sending alerts to all attendees asking them to check-in via the organization's methods
	Travel Contact	Provides information about the status of the airport and other travel methods
	Security Contact	Assesses current situation, provides guidance
	H.R. Contact	Begins monitoring the check-in process and who may need assistance
	Legal / Compliance Contact	Identifies legal responsibilities and processes that must be followed based on injuries
	IT Contact	Provides support on all technology needs
	Real Estate Contact	Provides information on the current status of office based on landlord reports and local information
	Finance Contact	Supports the people who may need financial assistance during the crisis
	Communications / PR Contact	Continually monitors all the incoming information and keeps attendees, travelers, employees, and media abreast of situation; responds to media request asking about number of deaths at hotel
	Hotel Supplier	Provides first-hand report on the damage to property and information from emergency personnel who are arriving on site
	Ground Transportation Supplier	Provides report as to how many people took advantage of the ground transportation, where they went, and the names of attendees

		Rental Car Supplier	Provides report as to how many people took advantage of the rental cars and the names of people who rented cars
	11:30 a.m.	Conclusion of Role Play	Debrief

Step 3	**Respond**
	Hurricane actually does strike land. Was everyone ready?

Step 4	**Recovery**

Debrief

- Were the processes correct?
- Did we have enough resources to assist us?
- Were we missing any key roles and expertise?
- Did the technology work?
- Were we missing any key technology?
- Did we secure the money we needed?
- Did we have all the right suppliers in place?

MORE Books, Information, and Tools
by Debi and Susan

"Meeting and Event Planning Playbook: A Quick Reference Guide for Administrative Assistants and Coordinators" by Debi Scholar and Susan Losurdo, 2013, available on Amazon and iTunes

"Strategic Meetings Management: Your SMM Toolkit" by Debi Scholar, 2013, available on Amazon and iTunes

"Strategic Meetings Management: The Strategy Quick Reference Guide" by Debi Scholar, 2010, available on Amazon and iTunes

The following tools and articles are available at www.TEPlus.net, all published by Debi Scholar.

2013

"Strategic Meetings Management: Master Hotel Contracts"

"Meetings Management Technology: An RFP for Services"

"62 Opportunities to Save Money on Meetings and Events"

"Meeting Management Company Pricing Secrets and Toolkit"

"Powerful Meeting Policy Toolkit"

"Do it Yourself for Service Level Agreements and Key Performance Indicators" aka "DIY for SLAs and KPIs"

2012

"Strategic Meetings Management: An RFP for Services"

"Creating a Virtual Meeting and Event Strategy"

"Demystifying Return on Investment (ROI) in meetings and events"

"Hotel Contracts in an SMM Environment: A Contracting Maturity Model"

"Strategic Meetings Management Business Plan"

2011

"Measuring the Value of the 7 Types of Meetings"

"Capture Regulatory Compliance Data in Meetings and Events"

"Develop a Compliance Strategy"

"Strategic Meetings Management: The History by Debi Scholar,"

"Getting a Baseline for your Current State Meetings Analysis"

"What is the Cost of Change?"

"Meeting Technology: Is it designed for Meeting Planners or Meeting Directors?"

"Travel Managers: Don't forget Group Travel"

"Strategic Meetings Management Presentation"

"Strategic Meetings Management: Become a Performance and Value Consultant"

"How Long Does it Take to Plan a Meeting?"

"The Return on Investment (ROI) in Meetings and Events"

"Strategic Meetings Management: Putting Yourself in Their Shoes: 35+ Questions for Stakeholders"

"Virtual Meetings and Events: The 20+ Roles and Responsibilities of the Virtual Meeting Planner".

"Strategic Meetings Management: 20 Questions to Choose the Right Resource Model"

2010

"40 Meeting Complexity Factors"

"Benchmark Your Strategic Meetings Management Program"

"Strategic Meetings Management Range Anxiety"

"Strategic Meetings Management: 80 Components to a Meetings Policy"

"Travel and Meetings: Use Change Management to Drive Compliance"

"Strategic Meetings Management: Maturity Model and Strategy Articulation Map"

"Benefits of Outsourcing Meetings and Events"

"20 Reasons to Consider Virtual Meetings"

"How to Negotiate your Corporate Card Terms"

"Strategic Meetings Management is Poetry to my Ears"

"T&E Fraud and the Impact on Your Business"

"15 Questions to Begin a Business Case"

2009

"Corporate Social Responsibility in Travel and Meetings"

"T&E Leading and Lagging Controls"

"Virtual Meetings: Eight Motivating Factors"

"Examine 13 Areas for Travel and Expense Management Optimization"

"Where do you find T&E Spend?"

"Demand Transparency in Pricing Models"

"Conduct Rate Audits to Reduce Costs"

"Use an Airline Analysis to Determine a Mix of Preferred Airlines"

"Request to all Internal Auditors: Please review Meetings and Events"

"What is Meeting Architecture?"

"How much is a Relationship Worth? Travel ROI"

"Corporate Dining may Represent 9% of T&E Spend"

"Career Ideas for e-Learning Instructional Designers"

How to find Debi and Susan:

Debi's blog, T&E Plus (www.TEPlus.net) has been viewed over 40,000 times as of early 2013 and provides information on archived webinars, tools, and guidance on meetings, travel, card and expense management.

Debi started the popular LinkedIn Group titled, "T&E Plus," which has over 2,500 members as of early 2013.

Debi started the popular LinkedIn Group titled "GBTA Strategic Meetings Management Group," which has over 1,000 members as of early 2013.

Debi created the industry's first free Strategic Meetings Management (SMM) Benchmark tool that allows you to score your current SMM operations at www.SMMBenchmark.com.

Debi's LinkedIn Profile is at www.linkedin.com/in/dscholar/.

Susan's LinkedIn Profile is at www.linkedin.com/in/slosurdo.